INDO-PACIFIC
BOTTLENOSE DOLPHIN
Tursiops aduncus

☑ **W9-BNN-615**

HUMAN
Homo sapiens

BLACK-BILLED
MAGPIE
Pica hudsonia

SHORT-FINNED
PILOT WHALE
*Globicephala
macrorhynchus*

MOUNTAIN
GORILLA
*Gorilla beringei
beringei*

BONOBO
Pan paniscus

RIDGEFIELD LIBRARY
472 MAIN STREET
RIDGEFIELD, CT 06877
(203) 438-2282
www.ridgefieldlibrary.org

JUL 1
2020

A Last
Goodbye

*For all of my family and friends—human and other species—who make my life so
rich and our goodbyes bittersweet.*

—EK

To my most favorite person in the universe, my dad, who became the stars in the sky.

*And to everyone who made this book come to life: Elin K, Mary Beth L, Alisa B,
Karen L, Karen B, and the Owlkids family.*

밤하늘의 별이 된 아빠에게.

—SK

Text © 2020 Elin Kelsey
Illustrations © 2020 Soyeon Kim

All rights reserved. No part of this publication may be reproduced, stored in a retrieval system, or
transmitted in any form or by any means, without the prior written permission of Owlkids Books Inc.,
or in the case of photocopying or other reprographic copying, a license from the Canadian Copyright
Licensing Agency (Access Copyright). For an Access Copyright license, visit www.accesscopyright.ca
or call toll-free to 1-800-893-5777.

Owlkids Books acknowledges the financial support of the Canada Council for the Arts, the Ontario
Arts Council, the Government of Canada through the Canada Book Fund (CBF) and the Government
of Ontario through the Ontario Creates Book Initiative for our publishing activities.

Published in Canada by
Owlkids Books Inc.
1 Eglinton Avenue East
Toronto, ON M4P 3A1

Published in the United States by
Owlkids Books Inc.
1700 Fourth Street
Berkeley, CA 94710

Library of Congress Control Number: 2019947223

Library and Archives Canada Cataloguing in Publication

Title: A last goodbye / written by Elin Kelsey ; artwork by Soyeon Kim.
Names: Kelsey, Elin, author. | Kim, Soyeon, illustrator.
Identifiers: Canadiana 20190141379 | ISBN 9781771473644 (hardcover)
Subjects: LCSH: Death—Juvenile literature. | LCSH: Bereavement—
Juvenile literature. | LCSH: Bereavement—Psychological aspects—Juvenile literature. | LCSH:
  Mourning customs—Juvenile literature.
Classification: LCC HQ1073.3 .K45 2020 | DDC j155.9/37—dc23

Edited by Mary Beth Leatherdale
Designed by Alisa Baldwin

Photography by Michael Cullen, TPG Digital Art Services

Manufactured in Shenzhen, Guangdong, China, in October 2019, by WKT Co. Ltd.
Job #19CB1393

A   B   C   D   E   F

ONTARIO ARTS COUNCIL
CONSEIL DES ARTS DE L'ONTARIO
an Ontario government agency
un organisme du gouvernement de l'Ontario

Canada Council
for the Arts

Conseil des Arts
du Canada

Canadä

OWL kids   Publisher of Chirp, Chickadee and OWL   Owlkids Books is a division of   bayard canada
www.owlkidsbooks.com

Written by
Elin Kelsey

A Last
Goodbye

Artwork by
Soyeon Kim

Owlkids Books

When it comes time to say
   our last goodbye,
I will wrap my trunk around you
   and support you with my tusks.

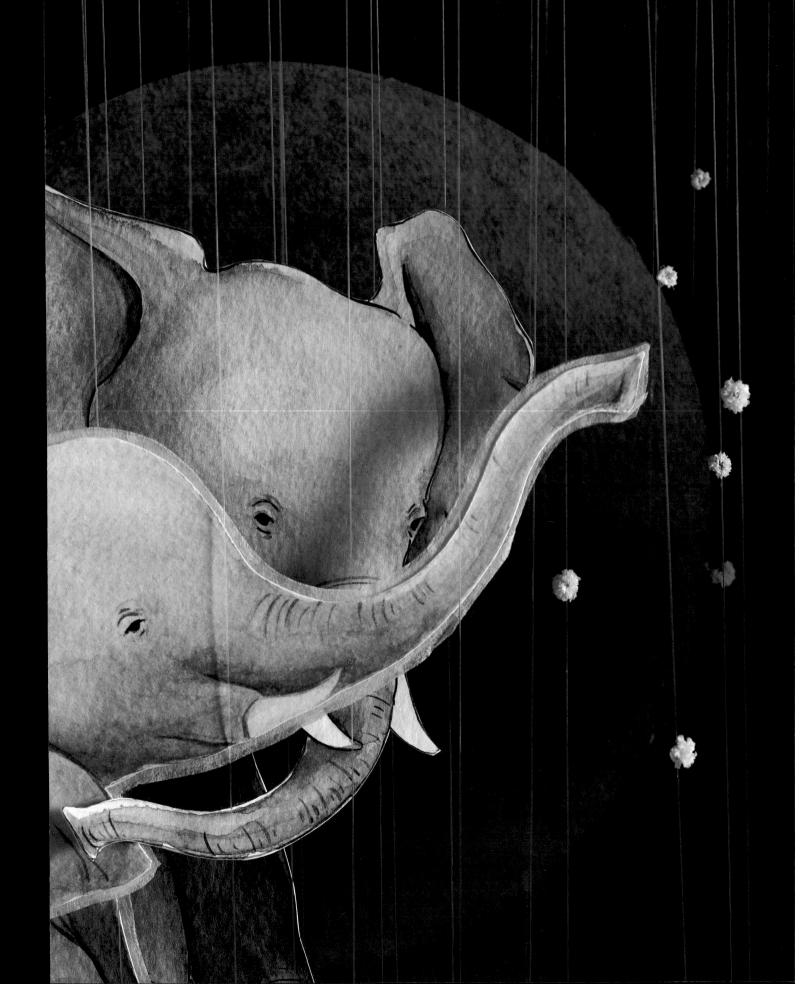

I will pump my powerful tail
and lift you to the surface,
where you can catch your breath.

I will tuck soft bedding behind your back

and carefully tend to your hair.

When it comes time to say
our last goodbye,

I will not want to leave you.

I will hold your hand.

I will gently hug and help you.

And when you die,

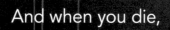

I will tenderly stroke
your body,

lie down beside you,

and keep you close.

I will cry out in sorrow,

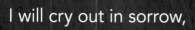

hold you tight,

or watch in quiet sadness.

After you die,

friends and family
will gather.

Some will travel
long distances

and stay for
many hours.

Others will place wreaths

or drape you in a blanket of forest green.

We will visit the place
    where your body rests.

What gifts will it share
as it settles into the earth?

Will tiny roots take hold
and tall trees grow
in the rich soil you nourish?

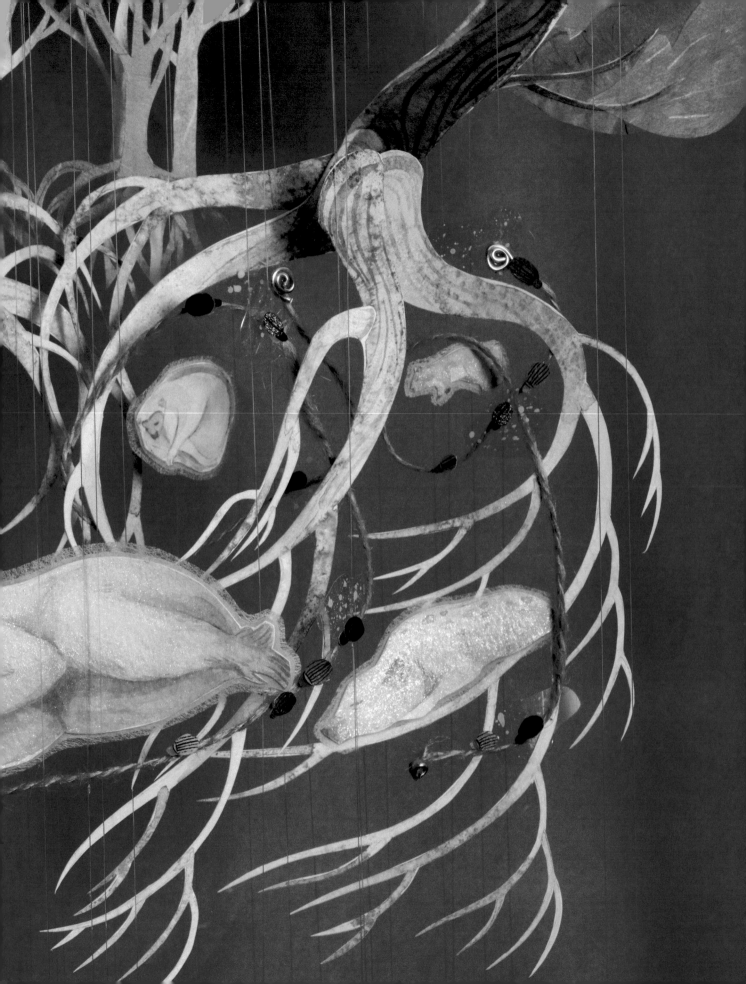

Will new undersea communities flourish

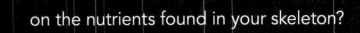

on the nutrients found in your skeleton?

I will miss you forever.

Yet, one day
soon,
I will think of you and feel joy.

I will remember you in the places
you loved to nap.

And sometimes I will be sad
and wish I could play with you.

Long after our last goodbye,
I will watch our children grow up.
I will watch our grandchildren, too.

They will look like us,

You,

me,

all of us.

Every species on Earth.

Our lives plant a long line of love

in this wild, thriving
planet.

A note from the author

While I was visiting a school for an author reading, a young girl named Avery stopped me in the playground to tell me that her dog had just died. "You have to stay with them and comfort them if you can," she said. "They are part of your family."

I appreciated Avery's wise words. When someone you care about is very sick or dying, it matters a lot. You might feel scared or angry or have trouble believing it's true. You might want to snuggle close or step away and do the things you normally do in your everyday life. Grief can make you feel lots of different ways.

Many animals express grief and care for each other at the end of life, too. When I was researching this book, I talked to scientists about how elephants, killer whales, and other highly intelligent, social animals that are featured in *A Last Goodbye* deal with death. They showed me videos and photos of animals mourning when someone close to them died. Every example in this book comes from that research.

Losing someone you love is a natural but painful part of life, whether you are an elephant, a dog, a chimpanzee, a whale, or a human. *A Last Goodbye* is a celebration of the ways in which people and many animals are there for one another in times when they are needed most. I find it beautiful and comforting to think of all the tender touches happening across the planet as trunks and fingertips and flippers stretch out to offer support. And that is why I wanted to share this book with you.

Warm thoughts,

Elin

P.S. To find out more about the science behind this book, be sure to visit:
www.owlkidsbooks.com/alastgoodbye